The Gay Debate
Stanton L. Jones

A note about the title: "The gay debate" is a phrase currently in common usage. In the gay community the term gay is used only to refer to men. The discussion of this booklet, however, applies to both gay men and lesbians.

InterVarsity Press
P.O. Box 1400, Downers Grove, IL 60515-1426
World Wide Web: www.ivpress.com
E-mail: mail@ivpress.com

©1994 by Stanton L. Jones

All rights reserved. No part of this book may be reproduced in any form without written permission from InterVarsity Press.

InterVarsity Press® is the book-publishing division of InterVarsity Christian Fellowship/USA®, a student movement active on campus at hundreds of universities, colleges and schools of nursing in the United States of America, and a member movement of the International Fellowship of Evangelical Students. For information about local and regional activities, write Public Relations Dept., InterVarsity Christian Fellowship/USA, 6400 Schroeder Rd., P.O. Box 7895, Madison, WI 53707-7895, or visit the IVCF website at <www.intervarsity.org>.

All Scripture quotations, unless otherwise indicated, are taken from the Holy Bible, New International Version®. NIV®. *Copyright ©1973, 1978, 1984 by International Bible Society. Used by permission of Zondervan Publishing House. All rights reserved.*

ISBN-10: 0-87784-093-8
ISBN-13: 978-0-87784-093-0

Printed in the United States of America ∞

P	14	13	12	11	10	9	8	7	6	5	4
Y	14	13	12	11	10	09	08	07	06		

When I confront the issue of homosexuality, I immediately think of the theology of human sexuality, of Christian sexual ethics, of matters of church order and of many related matters of principle and theology. But to think about homosexuality is to think also about people, some of whom I have known as acquaintances and a few well enough to love.

I think of Tom, who begged me to help him regain his Christian faith and stop his compulsive pursuit of anonymous sexual encounters and seductions of vulnerable teenage boys. Before I had a chance to really know him, Tom announced that he did not want to control himself any longer. Tom later wrote me in shocking and angry detail of his total immersion into the rough world of promiscuous oral and anal sex in the gay bathhouses and alleys of San Francisco. Tom is now dead of AIDS.

I think of Gail, a lesbian in a monogamous relationship, who speaks with passion of her Christian faith but who worships a god who accepts and affirms the "god force" within us all. She argues that the true Christian faith does not get bogged down in repentance and forgiveness but is empowered by love of any kind. Gail felt that her lesbianism should not entail a denial of her right to experience motherhood. She had several friends donate sperm so she could be artificially inseminated with no ties to a father. Gail gave birth to a baby whom she loves deeply.

I think of Fred, who was molested in puberty by an older brother. He subsequently threw himself for six years into a highly promiscuous gay subculture. He experienced no attraction to women. When Christ claimed his life, he immediately forsook his homosexual behavior in simple obedience to what he perceived to be the call of God. After a couple of years of costly discipleship and growth, Fred felt called by God to marry. His fiancée, Debbie, had full knowledge of his problem. Only toward the end of their engagement did Fred begin to experience any sexual attraction to Debbie. Now, after fourteen years of marriage, much prayer and counseling, Fred feels almost completely healed of his homosexual inclinations. He has little sexual attraction to men anymore, feels normal sexual attraction toward his wife, and feels that the heart of his homosexual struggle was a desperate longing for the love and affirmation of his father and a deep insecurity and doubt about his own manhood.

I think of Peter, who got involved with homosexual experimentation at a seventh-grade Bible camp. This early experience confirmed his suspicion that he was different. His high-school and college years were filled with furtive homosexual experiences followed by agonized repentance, prayer and weeks or months of trying to deny his homosexual feelings. He married Denise at the end of college, never telling her of his homosexual feelings and secretly hoping that the sexual experiences of marriage would cause his homosexual attractions to go away. Fifteen years later, when Denise discovered evidence of his homosexual affairs, both of their lives blew apart. Peter is now living in the gay community, feeling that he made every possible effort to change and that his calling now is to live as a gay Christian man in a monogamous gay relationship, though he has yet to achieve that monogamous relationship and no longer goes to church. Denise is consumed with rage and feels utterly betrayed. In retrospect, she believes that Peter's entire life has been a lie to himself and an attempt to manipulate others, and that he never made a serious attempt at repentance or change.

I also think of Mark, a single Christian businessman. He has known of his homosexual inclinations ever since he has been aware of any sexual feelings whatsoever. In his mid-twenties, Mark sporadically acted out his homosexual feelings in adult bookstores and public washrooms; he looks back on these experiences with a mixture of shame, revulsion and lust. The depth of Mark's commitment to Christ and costly discipleship is staggering to me. Mark has not acted on his homosexual wishes for over fifteen years now. But his pain is enormous. He often feels that he lives a twilight existence in the church, a church that does not know how to relate to single people, a church that acts in revulsion to the very idea of someone being homosexual, a church where he is pestered repeatedly as to why he does not marry, a church in which he longs for intimate fellowship but in which the chances of true honesty are few and far between.

These are the faces before me as I consider a Christian response to homosexuality—a response that involves answering three key questions: What is the Christian position on homosexuality and why? Why is it an important issue? And how should we live out our response?

The Christian Position on Homosexuality
When asked why they think homosexual behavior is wrong, many sincere Christians reply simply, "Because the Bible says it is!" The Bible does indeed condemn homosexual acts every time they are mentioned. But many Christians are unprepared for the revisionists' rejection of all of the major biblical texts as irrelevant or as misinterpreted. Following is a thumbnail sketch of what you will hear from a critic of the traditional view:

☐ The Leviticus 18:22 and 20:13 and Deuteronomy 23:18 passages which condemn male homosexual behavior are irrelevant, because they occur in the midst of a discussion of God's disapproval of the fertility cult worship practiced in the pagan communities surrounding the Israelites. The only kind of homosexual behavior the Israelites knew, it is argued, was homosexual prostitution in pagan temples. That is what is being rejected here, not the loving, monogamous gay relationships of persons of homosexual orientation today.

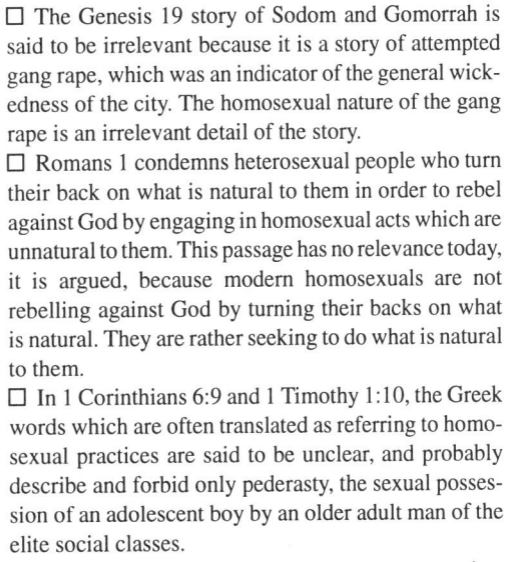

☐ The Genesis 19 story of Sodom and Gomorrah is said to be irrelevant because it is a story of attempted gang rape, which was an indicator of the general wickedness of the city. The homosexual nature of the gang rape is an irrelevant detail of the story.

☐ Romans 1 condemns heterosexual people who turn their back on what is natural to them in order to rebel against God by engaging in homosexual acts which are unnatural to them. This passage has no relevance today, it is argued, because modern homosexuals are not rebelling against God by turning their backs on what is natural. They are rather seeking to do what is natural to them.

☐ In 1 Corinthians 6:9 and 1 Timothy 1:10, the Greek words which are often translated as referring to homosexual practices are said to be unclear, and probably describe and forbid only pederasty, the sexual possession of an adolescent boy by an older adult man of the elite social classes.

These points make up a common argument against the Bible's condemnation of homosexuality. Let me speak back to those voices. Some of these criticisms have an element of legitimacy, but most biblical scholars concur that every one of them goes too far. The critics are right, for instance, in dismissing the view that homosexuality was the most heinous sin of Sodom and Gomorrah. Ezekiel 16:49-50 says, "Now this was the sin of your sister Sodom: She and her daughters were arrogant, overfed and unconcerned; they did not help the poor and needy. They were haughty and did detestable things before me. Therefore I did away with them as you have seen." Materialistic upper- and middle-class America may be more like Sodom than the modern gay community and closer to God's harsh judgement. We are quick to condemn those we are uncomfortable with and slow to judge ourselves.

Yet we cannot dismiss the sexual sin of Sodom and Gomorrah as irrelevant, because Scripture itself describes the sexual immorality of those cities (2 Peter 2:7; Jude 7). Moreover, Leviticus, Romans, 1 Corinthians and 1 Timothy *are* relevant and binding. Archaeological studies confirm that the ancient world knew of homosexual desire and practice, even if the concept of a psychological orientation was not present. Many different types of homosexual behavior were flagrantly practiced. In light of that truth, it is striking that *every time homosexual acts are mentioned in the Scriptures, they are condemned*. Make no mistake: the biblical witness against homosexual behavior can be neutralized only by either grossly misinterpreting the Bible or moving away from a high view of Scripture.[1]

Important as they are, I don't regard these passages as the cornerstone of the Christian stance that homosexual action is immoral. The core of the traditional Christian position on homosexual practice is rather the entire Christian vision of sexuality. This vision of sexuality applies equally to all, to homosexual persons and heterosexual, men and women, adult and child, all of us. As we examine this vision, I want to challenge every reader to live by a higher standard.

To have a truly Christian view of our own sexuality, we have to get first things first. There are four major acts in God's drama, this great epic poem of God's saving work in human life. We destroy our understanding of the script if we mix up the order of the acts. Act 1 is the creation; if we do not understand ourselves *first* as divine handiwork created in God's image, and understand God's creational intent for his works, everything else will be distorted. Act 2 is the Fall. Much of contemporary liberal scholarship emphasizes creation and denies the Fall. We must remember, however, that the Fall twists and ruins everything, but does not destroy the imprint of creation. Act 3 is redemption in and through Christ. Christ is at work in those who love him, redeeming them and redeeming the world. Act 4 is glorification, the expected final consummation, the blessed hope.

One place where this order of creation-fall-redemption is clearly reflected is 1 Timothy 4:1-5. Paul was dealing with heresies that denied creation, exaggerated the Fall and distorted the proper view of redemption. The Gnostics in particular distorted the proper view of sex, and that is exactly why Paul was trying to set Timothy and his people straight about the Christian view of marriage. The Gnostics despised marriage because they saw sex as evil. To this, Paul said:

> The Spirit clearly says that in later times some will abandon the faith and follow deceiving spirits and things taught by demons. Such teachings come through hypocritical liars, whose consciences have been seared as with a hot iron. They forbid people to marry and order them to abstain from certain foods, which God created to be received with thanksgiving by those who believe and who know the truth. For everything God created is good, and nothing is to be rejected if it is received with thanksgiving, because it is consecrated by the word of God and prayer.

How does this apply to sex? What did God make sex and marriage for? Paul's grounding is that God created

11

marriage; God created sex. Everything God created is good. But notice that what God created to be good has to be cleaned off; it has been dropped in the mud—that is the Fall. Through Christ, sex can be redeemed; that is what consecration means. Sex and marriage can be consecrated by being received with thanksgiving through the Word of God and prayer. We must start with creation, recognize the Fall and participate in redemption.

The heart of Christian sexual morality is this: God made sexual union for a purpose—the uniting of husband and wife into one flesh in marriage. God uses sexual intercourse, full sexual intimacy, to weld two people together (1 Corinthians 6:16). God has a big purpose in mind for sex because he has a big purpose for marriage—something bigger than for us to get our sexual needs met, have fun, have kids and not have to be lonely.

Look at what Ephesians 5 says about the purpose of marriage. Marriage is to model concretely here on earth what God wants in the relationship between Christ and his bride, the church. Jesus is one with the Father, and tells us that we can be one with him. We are utterly different from God, but he wants to unite with us (1 Corinthians 6:17). This reality can be uniquely modeled on earth through the union of two different kinds of human beings, male and female. Marriage is a living parable, a concrete symbol. And sexual intercourse is a life-uniting act that participates in the formation of a marriage. Each marriage can model for the world the mystical union of Christ and his people. Marriages have grand, even cosmic meanings in God's creational intent. And this grand meaning stands, regardless of how pathetically short we fall of that grand design.

Interestingly, scientific evidence supports this. If it is God's creational intent that sexual intercourse is meant to bond two people together for life in marriage and to participate in the creation of oneness in marriage, what would we expect the effect of premarital sex and cohabitation to be? Those actions should make marriage less likely to work. And that is what the facts show, especially in a recent study reported by Andrew Greeley in his book *Faithful Attraction*. People who have more premarital sex are more likely to have affairs in marriage, are less likely to have optimal sexual relationships in marriage and are likely to be less satisfied and happy with their marriages. Numerous studies over decades have shown that people who live together before marriage are more likely to divorce. All of the ways we humans foul up God's design have long-term negative consequences.

If marriage occupies this place in God's plan for all of life, and if sex is so important in God's plan for marriage, we can see the vital importance of obedience to God's standards for sexuality. Sex is a gift, but it is a gift we can abuse. God's intent is that sex be used rightly inside and outside of marriage. Inside of marriage, it is to be shared lovingly and with gratitude to build up the unity and oneness of the couple. Outside of the marriage of a man and woman, the proper use of sex is to honor God by costly obedience in living a chaste life and to learn through the difficulties this presents to value obedience over gratification, to value serving God over serving our own lusts, and to find God to be the only source that truly meets our needs. For the heterosexual or the homosexual, the call of Christ is the same—if you find yourself unmarried, God wants you to live a chaste life.

But isn't this unfair to the homosexual person? The heterosexual single at least has the chance of marriage. The person with homosexual longings has no such chance. He did not choose to have the feelings and inclinations he does. Is it fair to Mark to argue that God is calling him to a life of chaste singleness? Is it fair to

Gail to suggest that God would have her forgo motherhood because she is not married?

First, let's acknowledge that few people *choose* to have homosexual inclinations. The evidence suggests that genetic factors, possibly operative through brain differences, may give some a push in the direction of homosexual preference. Disordered family relationships that leave people confused and uncertain at a deep level about their sexual identity seem to play a major role as well. Early homosexual experiences of seduction or abuse may also play a role, as the stories of Fred and Peter illustrated earlier. And many lesbians, especially, seem to have been the targets of sexual abuse by men earlier in life, leaving them with deeply impaired abilities to trust or feel close to men.

But the existence of inclinations, orientations or preferences has little to do with God's moral call upon our lives. Social science is finding many powerful factors which shape character and influence morally laden choices. Alcoholism, anxiety-proneness, ill-temperedness, and even the propensity to violence and victimization are made more likely by the presence of certain genetic and family variables. Is it unfair then for God to hold up sobriety and moderation, trust and faith, self-control and patience, restraint and respect as moral values?

No, because God is the Maker, the One who sets the design. And though God is perfectly just, God never promised to be fair by mere human standards. We are saved by grace, but in the race that Paul talks about, the race to press on to the high calling of Christ, some of us start further back in the pack than others, further back from the ideal. But that does not make the goals that God ordains illegitimate or nonbinding. While one ideal, heterosexual marriage, is not an option for the homosexual Christian without a large dose of divine healing, the other ideal, chaste singleness, is open and accessible. And that ideal of chaste singleness holds out the possibility of true integrity and beauty, as the models of Jesus himself, Paul and many other saints show. The fact that such chastity is difficult for homosexual persons is of little moral consequence, as it is also difficult for heterosexuals. The difficulty should be dealt with pastorally, not by changing the moral standard.

And so the Christian vision for sexuality and marriage is our foundational reason for rejecting homosexual action as a legitimate moral option. A warning, though: many gay Christians will simply deny that this is the binding Christian view. Many advocates of a liberalization of the church's ethical stance suggest that the only imperative of the Bible or of the Christian tradition that is binding upon all people is the general call to manifest sacrificial love, honesty and so forth. Gay relationships, it is argued, can do this as well as straight.

The first problem with this argument is that it does not truthfully reflect the Christian tradition. It is ultimately irrelevant whether homosexual couples can be just as loving, faithful, monogamous or whatever as heterosexual couples. God has a distinctive purpose for sex and for marriage.

Second, the revisionist's argument simply doesn't match reality. For example, male homosexuality tends to be strongly associated with promiscuity: The famous Bell and Weinberg study *(Homosexualities)* suggested that about a third of gays have had over 1,000 sexual partners in their lifetimes. Very few gays are in committed, long-term relationships; Bell and Weinberg found that under 10% of gays are in such relationships. Those who are in stable relationships do not tend to be sexually monogamous. McWhirter and Mattison *(The Gay Couple)* found that 0% of the 100 stable male couples they studied were sexually monogamous after being together for five years. The authors of that study, a gay couple themselves, said that to be gay is to be nonmonogamous and that monogamy is an unnatural state that some gay men attempt because of their internalized homophobia, so that when gay men finally grow to accept their gayness, they shed monogamy like a butterfly sheds a cocoon.

It may be that so many in the homosexual community do not or cannot embrace monogamy because homosexual sex can never produce what God made sex for. They instead turn to promiscuity and perversions to create sexual highs. The gay community calls these perversions "high-tech sex." Many know of oral and anal sex, but fewer know of commonly, though not universally, practiced activities such as sadomasochistic practices of inflicting pain on a partner during sex, group sex of all kinds, and more extreme distortions. When sex outside of God's will does not do what God made it to do, many people, gay and straight, search for some way to make sex deliver an ever bigger electric charge, the elusive ultimate orgasm that can somehow make up for the absence of what sex was meant to create: unity between two different kinds of people—a man and a woman.

In summary, persons of homosexual inclination are under the same moral call as we all are—to respond to the offer of divine mercy and forgiveness through the gift of Jesus Christ, and to offer back our lives as the only gift we can give in return. If we love him, we will obey his commands. And his will with regard to our sexuality is either that we live chaste lives of dependence upon him or that we strive to build a marriage that models Christ's love for the church before the watching world, aided by the uniting gift of sexual intercourse. All of us should strive anew to live by this holy standard.

Why Is This an Important Issue?

Homosexual acts are just like every other sin: they violate God's express will and they distort God's creational design. There ought to be just as much or more fire coming from our church pulpits against greed, pride, racism, arrogance, lack of compassion and spiritual lukewarmness as against homosexual action. The best estimates today suggest that at most 2 to 3 percent of the population engage in homosexual acts (*not* the 10 percent or more that badly biased research once suggested). In that light, why should homosexuality be a special concern today?

There are three reasons that it must be a special concern, and none of them has anything to do with homosexual people being especially bad or disgusting (because they are not). First, the historically high Christian view of the authority of Scripture is threatened by efforts at revision. As I said before, the biblical witness against homosexual behavior can be neutralized only by either grossly misinterpreting the Bible or by moving away from a high view of Scripture. And that is exactly what the apologists for the gay Christian movement do.

While claiming to be staunchly within the Christian tradition, revisionists terribly distort biblical sexual ethics. Chris Glasser, writing in the Presbyterian tradition, says in his book *Come Home! Reclaiming Spirituality and Community as Gay Men and Lesbians* that fidelity doesn't mean being sexually exclusive and monogamous; fidelity really only means keeping your promises. So if the gay Christian companion promises to only have five other lovers per year, he is being faithful if he stays in those limits.

Episcopal biblical scholar William Countryman, in *Dirt, Greed and Sex*, adopts a biblical theology that allows for homosexual practice, but he has the courage to admit that his method of interpretation also makes prostitution and sex with animals legitimate options for the Christian (as long as such acts are done in love).

In her book *Touching Our Strength,* Carter Heyward, an Episcopal ethicist, suggests that heterosexual marriage enslaves women. She calls instead for loving sexual friendships; and there is no reason to limit these life-giving "godding" relationships to only one person or to one sex.

The majority group of the Presbyterian Special Committee on Sexuality, which authored *Presbyterians and Human Sexuality, 1991,* claimed that God's Word to us is those parts within the Bible which are just and loving, which liberate people and make them more satisfied and fulfilled; the rest of the Bible is simply not God's Word. Therefore, the group argued, a prohibition against sex outside of marriage oppresses and frustrates single people and denies their sexual rights, so that could not be God's Word.

The second reason homosexuality is an important issue is that what the Bible treats as an isolated *act* to be condemned (namely, people of the same gender having sex) our society treats as a fundamental element of personal *identity*. In this view, the people I described at the beginning of this booklet are not people who engaged in certain acts or who have certain inclinations. Instead, they *are* homosexuals, gay people. Their sexual inclinations define their very being. If a sexual desire defines the very person, then acting on that desire is essential to personhood. If we accept this logic, then to suggest that God does not want them to engage in homosexual acts is to insult their innermost beings.

What is our Christian response to this? We must deny that it is legitimate to define persons by their sexual desires, or any other fallen element of human nature. In Christ, our identities are to be formed by our adoption as his children, and our character is to be formed by the cultivation of the moral virtue that he desires for us.

Romans 6:16 teaches us that we don't just find or discover our selves; we also form our selves. We build a moral and personal momentum by the choices we make. We are progressively becoming either more a slave to sin or a greater slave to Christ. If what you mean by saying you are a homosexual is that you experience homosexual desire, that is reality. If what you mean by saying you are homosexual is that your identity is defined by your gayness and that living out those sexual leanings is essential to your very nature, then your identity is misplaced; you are trying to build an identity on shifting sand. For this reason Christians must continue striving to love the sinner but hate the sin, even though this saying drives the gay Christian community crazy. We can say this and strive for this because we refuse to make homosexual behavior or preference the core of anyone's identity.

The third reason this issue is vital today is that there is unrelenting pressure on the church to change its historic stance. This is presented as a simple issue: the church has evolved in rejecting slavery, racism and sexism, and now it is time to stop its most deeply entrenched bigotry—homohatred, heterosexism and homophobia. There is a problem here again, though: we can change our position only by changing our fundamental stance on biblical authority, changing our core view of sexuality and changing our conception of the meaning and character of Christ's call upon our lives. The first two I have already addressed; but more needs to be said on the nature of Christ's call.

Christ was our perfect model of love and compassion, and we have much to learn from his love for sinners and participation in their lives. But he didn't just ooze warm fuzzies; Christ also had the gall to tell others how to live their lives, to insist that his truth was the only truth and to claim that he alone was the way to God. In short, Jesus was what many people today would call a narrow-minded bigot.

And we, the church, have been entrusted with proclaiming the message that we have received from him. When we do, we risk being called rigid and narrow-minded. We must face the reality that Christianity "discriminates." It says one path is the right way. Christians make a ridiculous set of claims: that an omnipotent God bothered to create and love us, that he let us and our forebears spit in his face in rebellion, that he chose a peculiar and unsavory primitive tribe to be his conduit for blessing, that he actually revealed what he wanted these people to believe and how they were to live, and that this God actually became a person and died for us to conquer death on our behalf. That is a most unlikely story! But Christians are supposed to spread the news that this is *the* story, the only true story.

The church has, in each generation, been faced with new challenges that are new twists on old issues. The current challenge of homosexuality as an acceptable alternative lifestyle, of gay persons as a social group that must be loved and accepted as they are, is the newest form of an old set of challenges—the challenges to diminish the authority of God's revelation, to understand people on their own terms rather than by God's view of them and fundamentally to amend the nature of Christ's call to take up our crosses and follow him.

How Should We Respond?
In this difficult time, there are two things we must do. They are two things that do not naturally go together. We must exhibit the very love and compassion of Jesus Christ himself. And we must fearlessly proclaim the truth that Jesus Christ himself proclaimed and embodied.

Perhaps the key to compassion is to see ourselves in another, to see our common humanity. This is what many of us cannot or will not do. A certain degree of natural revulsion to homosexual acts per se is natural for heterosexuals. All of us should be thankful that there are at least some sinful actions to which we are not naturally drawn. But revulsion to an act is not the same as a revulsion to a person. If you cannot empathize with a homosexual person because of your fear of or revulsion to them, then you are failing our Lord. You are guilty of pride, fear or arrogance. And if you are causing others to stumble, you are tying a millstone around your own neck (Luke 17:1-2).

The homosexual people I know are very much like me. They want love, respect, acceptance, companionship, significance, forgiveness. Like those of us whose instincts tell us to acquire security through acquiring possessions or the approval of others, or like those of us who find it inconvenient and unnatural to care deeply about others, persons struggling with homosexuality desire the right thing at their core. But for reasons often beyond their control, they have come to seek those right things in the wrong ways.

We, the church, have the opportunity to speak, with our words and our lives, of God's own love for the homosexual person. If we truly love we will act on that love. We must start by eradicating our negative responses to homosexual people. We must stop the queer jokes and insults; they hurt others. We must deal with our own emotional reactions; we must decide to love. We must change the church to a place where the person who feels homosexual desire can be embraced. We must make the church a place where a repentant man or woman can share with another, with many, about the sexual desires he or she feels, and still receive prayerful support and acceptance.

Are you willing to pray with, eat with, hug and comfort, share life with a woman or man who has homosexual feelings? Frequently we already do but do not know it. Just as we share meals with gluttons, shop with the greedy, share compliments with the prideful and vegetate with the slothful—and as others share life with us without knowledge of our hidden sins—so also we already share life, knowingly or unknowingly, with the homosexual. But we need to do so knowingly and lovingly.

Now the second part of our call—to speak the truth. If we truly love, we will not shrink from speaking God's view of homosexual behavior. Don't be deceived—increasingly today we are defined as being unloving on the basis of viewing homosexuality as immoral, regardless of the compassion we exhibit. Be prepared to be labeled as an unloving bigot if you speak the truth. Nevertheless, strive to be truly loving when you do speak. Christian compassion does not mean acceptance of the gay lifestyle any more than it means affirming an adulterer's infidelity.

As people of homosexual inclination follow our Lord down the narrow road, they can pray and hope for healing. There are two prevalent distortions about healing today. The first is the conservative Christian myth that a quick, sincere repentance and prayer for healing will instantly change the person. Thankfully, few spread this damaging myth today. The more prevalent myth is the opposite, that there is no hope for healing.

Anyone who says there is no hope is either ignorant or a liar. Every secular study of change has shown some success rate, and persons who testify to substantial healing by God are legion. There is hope for substantial change for some in this life.

But while our ultimate hope is secure, we do not have certainty about how much healing and change are available for every homosexual person in this life. Some will never be healed of their homosexual orientation. We need to balance a Christian triumphalism with a theology of suffering, a recognition that we are a hurting and beaten-down race. We must not believe the world when it tells us there is an easy answer to everything, even when the speaker is a Christian. There is dignity and purpose in suffering. The Christian homosexual's witness is not invalidated by pain and difficulty; Christians trust that there is always a deeper purpose in suffering.

Mark, my Christian brother who stills longs for healing while he lives a life of celibacy, and many like him, needs to be assured by the church of the meaningfulness of his pilgrimage. We need to urge Mark and others like him to continue to struggle and hold fast, having Christ as their goal. Each of us can be a Christlike witness in how we bear our sufferings. A Christian witness is not found just in strength and triumph, but also in brokenness. We all want to be triumphant witnesses, but few of us are. For many of us, examined or unexamined pain lies very close to the surface behind the "glittering images" we show at church. Our homosexual brothers and sisters who follow our Lord in costly discipleship have much to teach all of God's people. And we all have much to learn about the proclamation of God's truth and about how to love those whose struggles are different from ours.

As a church, we should pray that our Father and Creator, who made us sexual beings in his own image, would give us grace to understand just how fearfully and wonderfully we are made. We need help to perceive in our sexual desires our incompleteness, brokenness and need for oneness with Christ. We need a vision for following Christ in costly discipleship. We need to learn respect for the marvelous gift of our sexuality and to use that gift in the way God intends. We need to be empowered to live chaste lives that bring glory to the Creator and to create godly marriages that reflect his truth.

We need to pray that God will give to those who struggle with homosexual desires a special measure of grace to be healed of those passions, and special grace to perceive the comforting presence of the Holy Spirit alongside them in their struggles and sufferings. We need to pray for greater strength to courageously proclaim the truth. Finally, we all need to repent of our arrogant, hateful and intolerant attitudes toward those whose struggles are uncomfortably different from ours, and move toward being the kind of community that embodies the welcoming grace and love of our Lord Jesus Christ.

---

[1]For a more detailed discussion of the biblical witness about homosexual behavior, see Thomas Scmidt, *Straight and Narrow?* (Downers Grove, Ill.: InterVarsity Press, 1995); Richard B. Hays, "Awaiting the Redemption of Our Bodies: The Witness of Scripture Concerning Homosexuality," *Sojourners* 20 (July 1991): 17-21; this excellent essay has been reprinted in *Homosexuality in the Church,* ed. Jeffrey S. Siker (Louisville, Ky.: Westminster/John Knox, 1994). See also appendix A in Bob Davies and Lori Rentzel, *Coming Out of Homosexuality: New Freedom for Men and Women* (Downers Grove, Ill.: InterVarsity Press, 1993).

About the Author
Stanton L. Jones is chair of the psychology department of Wheaton College, where he has been developing its doctoral program in clinical psychology. With Richard E. Butman, he coauthored Modern Psychotherapies: A Comprehensive Christian Appraisal. *His latest book, written with his wife, Brenna, is* How and When to Tell Your Kid About Sex: A Life-Long Approach to Shaping Your Child's Sexual Character *(NavPress).*

For More Information and Practical Help
Exodus International is a coalition of Christian ministries worldwide that provide support to men and women seeking to overcome homosexuality. These outreaches offer such services as support groups, one-on-one counseling, literature, newsletters and other helpful resources. For a free introductory packet of literature on Exodus, including a complete list of referral ministries, contact Exodus International, P.O. Box 2121, San Rafael, CA 94912; (415) 454-1017.